OBOE CLASSICS

FOR THE

INTERMEDIATE PLAYER

To access audio visit:
www.halleonard.com/mylibrary

Enter Code
8237-6638-7568-9889

ISBN 978-1-59615-359-2

EXCLUSIVELY DISTRIBUTED BY

HAL•LEONARD®

© 2007 MMO Music Group, Inc.
All Rights Reserved

Visit Hal Leonard Online at
www.halleonard.com

Contact us:
Hal Leonard
7777 West Bluemound Road
Milwaukee, WI 53213
Email: info@halleonard.com

In Europe, contact:
Hal Leonard Europe Limited
42 Wigmore Street
Marylebone, London, W1U 2RN
Email: info@halleonardeurope.com

In Australia, contact:
Hal Leonard Australia Pty. Ltd.
4 Lentara Court
Cheltenham, Victoria, 3192 Australia
Email: info@halleonard.com.au

CONTENTS

Dear Young Oboists and Teachers,

I compiled this second volume with the high-school oboist in mind. The selections span "Solos Level 3 and 4" (of 6 levels) in the New Jersey Regional Solo List. Some students will be ready for these pieces after 3 or 4 years of study (8th or 9th grade,) but they will be useful throughout high school, and they are significant enough to play on a professional recital. They are arranged progressively, the Hindemith Sonata presenting a great challenge to rhythm and counting. Imitation is one of the best ways to learn style and good taste, but if you have trouble reproducing something you hear, please refer to the booklet notes for musical and technical advice. It should be great fun to have a piano alone track for practice, and I hope the text will help illuminate my thought process. I would like to dedicate my work on this project to my teacher John Mack, who continues to challenge and inspire me and who instilled love and devotion for teaching. Special thanks also goes to Gail Warnaar of The Double Reed Shop, Barnet, Vermont, for helping me find and choose the repertoire.

—*Elaine Douvas*

Notes on the Music

Gabriele Pierné - Pièce in g minor

Style should be the main focus in this charming French work. An overall impression of imagination and fluency is the most important thing. The first theme has a mysterious, elfin quality, so the tone should have lots of animation, ring and clarity. Try for light, clear articulation with nice up-inflection of the two 8th notes, and give some rhythmic poise by sometimes holding back a little on these pick-up notes.

The staccato notes should be mostly tone with very little tongue noise. If they sound "spitty," I believe you have the ability to clarify the tone by the way you hold and focus the air. Here's something to think about: support is not how much you blow, but how you hold the air. You control and concentrate the air by holding it firmly between the abdominal muscles and a focusing place in the throat. It is sort of like putting your thumb over the end of the garden hose. If want to water the flowers six feet away, you wouldn't turn up the water full blast and knock all the petals off the flowers. You would keep the water amount moderate, and use your thumb to get a traveling, aerated stream. You can find this place in the throat by saying "young" (or by gargling!) You don't need much air to play the oboe, especially at a quiet volume. Blowing against yourself removes the sound of pressure at the reed, so it will sound floating, elevated and pure. The articulation will never be any clearer than the tone on which it is done!

The exuberant middle section needs a lot of singing quality. One of the most important things in playing any instrument is for it to sound vocal, that is, the way singers sing. There are many things that go into this, but first and foremost, the music must sound natural, smooth, flowing, and without mechanical interference (more on quiet finger action in the notes for *Elegiac Dance*.) Also try to order the dynamics in a vocal way: brilliant and full in the high notes and counteracting the oboe's tendency to "roar" in the low notes. When you practice scales, start very softly in the low register, crescendo to the fullest at the top of the scale, and diminuendo again to the bottom. This will build a good habit. This is the way a voice sings, and it's the natural way of music.

Use your left-F key if you have one, because the forked-F is usually too "wooly-sounding" to match the other notes. The long trill with the little finger is difficult. I am using a "double trill," that is, alternating the left and right Eb keys to get more speed.

Corelli-Barbirolli - Concerto for Oboe and Strings

Corelli (1653-1713) was a composer of the Baroque Period, the time of Bach. In 1947, the English conductor, Sir John Barbirolli, arranged some of Corelli's themes into this lovely concerto for his wife, the famous English oboist, Evelyn Rothwell.

The "Preludio" has great nobility and a beautiful singing quality; it is introspective and serene. Try to show the pleasing architectural shape of the melody. Whenever you have a spelled-out triad such as the first three notes of the piece, just match the dynamic to the position of the note in the scale: A-C-F would be 3-5-1. The C is the loudest, and the low F is the softest. This is the natural way of music and the absolute opposite of what will happen on the oboe, unless you make a conscious effort! Cs are notoriously thin and bare on the oboe. Make an exercise of B-C-B-C etc., trying to thicken and match the two tones. Keep experimenting until the C is the same color as the B and there is a small half-step of pitch. Go by ear, but you might try going to the tip of the reed, opening the jaws, and "over-loading" or funneling extra air against the focus in your throat. The opposition of lipping down and wind-ing up gives breadth and content to the tone. Don't let low F stick out.

In all Baroque music, whenever you have a trill on a dotted or tied note, try to stop the trill right on the tie, and replace the motion of the trill

with vibrato on the tie. The downward slurs need an arched, vocal shape (for elaboration, see the notes for the Nielsen Romance.)

The "Allemanda" is very lively and joyous. As in the first movement, please order the dynamics in the first theme according to the register: brilliant high notes, deeper, gentler low notes. The 8th notes should be detached and sturdy, but flexible like a bow-stroke (the notes taper a bit, like saying the syllable "m" on the ends.) Keep it spirited, bouncy and dance-like, with strong accents on beats 1 and 3.

The "Giga" (ZHEE ga) has a wonderful rhythmic swing. When you get to the mixed articulation, slur 2-tongue 2, take care that all the notes are equally heard and that the rhythm is unaffected by the slurred groups. These two rules apply to all mixed articulation, because the slurs tend to rush, and the notes that aren't tongued often sound weak. I refer you to the Barret Oboe Method preliminary articulation study no. 22 for practice; then melody no. 14, then the triplet solo from Rossini's Italian in Algiers. Don't shorten the end of the slurs, or the pattern will sound uneven.

G. P. Telemann - Andante and Presto

The mood of the Andante is regal, spacious, and elegant. Present the first note very grandly, with a lot of travel, like a fast length of bow. Lift and curve the end of the note as if pronouncing an "m" on the end. To play with the "inflections of speech" is another component of vocal style. Then play the half-note much softer, like an echo. In general, don't let the long notes stick out just because they are long; that would be "accidental syncopation." The stress in the phrase belongs on the first notes in each bar for this theme.

The pairs of 8th notes should have a flexible, lilting quality. The effect of the tonguing is to give forward direction and energy to the melodic line. Do not clip the slurs! A slur is just a bow-change on a string instrument and just a place to tongue for winds; it is not a "phrase mark." You can get a lifting effect by playing: loud-soft-loud-soft in the pairs, but if you clip them, it will sound too choppy! Beats 4, 5, and 6 should crescendo, leading forward with energy toward the downbeats. I love the rich and surprising harmony at m. 22. The climax at m. 23 and 24 should sound victorious!

In the Presto, an important point of style is that the quarter notes are mostly bouncy and lifted, but the ones that are followed by two 8ths should be longer. All of the quarter notes, whether short or long, should have a curve in them, as if you sang an "m" syllable on the ends. The pick-up notes should be short and energetic; this is also an essential part of Classical style.

In the mixed articulation, slur 3-tongue 1, don't forget the two rules (see Corelli notes): 1) all notes equally heard, and 2) rhythm unaffected by the slurred groups. I refer you to the Barret Oboe Method preliminary articulation study no. 9 to practice equalizing the tongued and slurred notes. The figure, "tongue 1-slur 3" is like a violin figure; you would use the same amount of bow on the tongued note as on the 3 slurred ones put together. Get a lot of travel in that single staccato note: a broad jump. Let it ring and sound open-ended, such as in Ferling no. 4 or Barret articulation study no. 11 (of the 12.)

The end is very dramatic with lots of expressive chromatic notes and a "cadenza!" Lean on the first of each pair in m. 55 and 56, then take a dramatic breath before G# and play the triplets freely—out of rhythm. This is the cadenza, a section meant to sound like free virtuoso improvisation. It should sound like you made it up on the spot!

In the Presto, we chose to play a tempo different from the printed metronome mark. Metronome marks are often by an editor rather than the composer, and you must use your own good judgment.

MICHAEL HEAD - ELEGIAC DANCE

Michael Head was the piano accompanist for the English oboist, Evelyn Rothwell Barbirolli. One day she said, "Why don't you try writing some music," and so he did. If you like these two inventive pieces, you can also play the *Gavotte* and the *Rondo* by Head. The *Elegiac Dance* (el uh JI ack) is poetic, penetrating, and deeply sincere. The mood expresses contemplative inward sorrow. A simple melody such as this is in danger of sounding "sing-song," that is, trite with a repetitious, monotonous accent on the beats. Try to elevate the melodic line by bringing out the notes between the main beats. Feel the beauty of the upper and lower neighbors (E♭ and C) in the 32nd note turning figure, and press on the expressive chromatic notes.

Continuity of line is extremely important here. Try to connect well the long notes with the start of the moving notes. Do not make a habit of lilting away in the long notes. The sustained line and melting "legato" must not be interrupted by awkwardness over the break (C to D) or by noisy straight fingers. Practice thickening the Cs so they can match a D (see the notes on the Corelli for directions on this.) Straight fingers can be heard as jagged, angular note changes. Take care that the fingers move quietly, sneakily, curved, with a gentle squeezing action. Try picking the fingers up a little before squeezing them down; if you keep them too close to the keys, the only way to get them down is to snap them. The oboe must cover well, so that the keys don't have to be hit for response.

The outpouring of emotion toward the high Ds should sound like a spontaneous flight of imagination, soaring and breaking out of the narrow confinement of the theme. Do something beautiful with the G octaves and fermata on D. I recommend slurring to high D with the left-hand index finger lifted. The half-hole key should be down for tonguing and up for slurring. If the half-hole key opens too far to make this work, screw it down a little.

The middle section, now in a major key, is more optimistic. Always be sure to react to changes of key ("modulation.") It must sound as though we've traveled to another land! The mood is now hopeful, wistful, and warmer. The rhapsodic group of eleven 16ths could be felt as 3+3+5. Try for your finest diminuendo at the end of the piece. (More on how to play softly in the notes for the Nielsen Romance.)

MICHAEL HEAD - PRESTO

The *Presto* makes a nice pair with the *Elegiac Dance* for a contest or a recital. This piece needs really sprightly tonguing with no pressure or "cracking" of attacks. What makes a note crack anyway? Cracking comes from one of two things: aiming the pitch at a place that is not the reed's natural center. or blowing too much air for the size of the reed's opening. This means you are blowing too hard, the reed is too closed, or you are closing the reed with your jaws. If the reed is flat, then you have to close your jaws to make the right pitch, but cracking of attacks will result. The best guarantee against cracking is to have a reed with excellent "pitch floor," a point below which the pitch cannot drop. Then you can open the jaws and voice down without being flat (and I mean the high notes too!) If you are making your own reeds, the pitch floor is a function of very tight sides and some "stoppage" behind a tip that is not too long. It is always a challenge to make a reed with a large opening (for color and dynamic range) that is totally up to pitch.

Concerning the "slur 2–tongue 2" articulation, in this case, please do clip the ends of the slurs to match the staccato notes that follow. The little "squiggle" (1st note, 2nd line) is an "inverted mordent" or "short trill." One "up and down," like a triplet on the beat, is all that is needed.

On page 2, line 3, when you see the confusing double set of slurs, the lower set is the actual tonguing. The long upper slur is a "phrase-mark," indicating that the tonguing should be smooth and unobtrusive, gently urging the tone forward with no gaps or "hiccups" at the tonguing junctures. Tongue late and fast with a clear, expressive "tee" or "tah" that does not stop the previous note.

CARL NIELSEN - ROMANCE

The *Romance* is an intense piece, full of contrasts and sudden turns of minor and major. In the first four bars, try to contrast the haunting melancholy, expressed in the sighing downward intervals, with the passionate confidence of the up-sweeping ones. "Con duolo" means with pain or grief, but don't let it sound too morbid. The mournful expression comes from the often repeated "tritone" intervals (augmented 4ths): the descending A♭-D, F#-C, and C#-G. This is the most dissonant interval in music, and it is so painful that you must take a little extra time to let it

register. Try singing it, and you will see that it takes extra time to sing dissonances or big leaps. This is another part of vocal style.

I'm sure you can feel expression and stress on m. 8 and m. 10, the dissonant C# and G#, resolving to D and A. Always bring out this feeling of stress and relief, and don't play all the notes with the same intensity. This dissonance has a name: the C# and G# are each an "appoggiatura," (uh pojya TOO ruh) that is, a note that doesn't fit with the chord of the moment, but it pulls strongly to the neighboring note that is in the harmony. We play these dissonances with expression and emphasis, then the resolution is felt as relief, repose. Ordinarily you would neither blow harder nor bite to play softly; there is no repose in that! The soft tone should sound open and ringing; it should not sound squeezed, bitten, muffled or missing its high overtones. To play softly, blow less air and adjust the "thumb over the garden hose" in your throat to keep the travel and compression in the tone. Don't bite the reed, or it will lose its color and ring, it won't respond to a smaller amount of air, and you'll be sharp on all of your diminuendos.

The downward slurs are really difficult in this piece and need your serious attention. First, make sure that your G is deeper than your A. Make an exercise of this: A-G-A-G, etc., making sure that the G is longer and deeper, "ee-oh-ee-oh," not "oh-aing-oh-aing." Don't even try D to G until the G is fixed! In order to sound vocal, the downward slurs need an active shape; don't just let them drop out. Try aiming upward instead of straight down at the note. The shape should be arched as if going over a waterfall: out first, then down. Bring the air to a crest at the end of the upper note. Then, at the last moment before changing notes, practically stop blowing as you go to the lower note. This gets a lot of content in the interval or "portamento" (Italian for "carried over,") and it is very singing.

I would suggest tonguing the first of the pair of grace-notes in the second to the last line. Indeed, most grace-notes sound better tongued for clarity, because they are harmonically interesting, and to prevent them from sounding like a dotted rhythm.

CARL NIELSEN - HUMORESQUE

Crisp, clean tonguing is essential to the jolly, witty mood in the *Humoresque*. On the pairs of 16ths and on the pair of 32nds, play two distinct, equally short notes. I refer you to the Barret Oboe Method, melodies 11, 12, and 13 to practice this. This is jaunty, spirited music! Another help to the rhythmic swing is to curve each of the eighth notes before the pair of 16ths. Don't play with a straight tone here. Also curve the big syncopation on C right before the double bar. After all, syncopation comes for the Latin "syncopare," meaning to "faint or swoon."

When you get to the continuous tonguing, make sure it is "on point," light, clean, and up-inflected. No matter how short a note is, always get a full cross-section of the tone: no cracking! In the words of my former teacher, John Mack, "It's like the meat slicer at the deli: no matter how paper thin the slice, it's always a full cross-section, complete with the rim of fat around the outside." We want articulation that takes nothing away from the tone; think 98% tone to 2% tongue noise. Be sure the tips of the reed are in the clear—no lip on the tips, or you will get blunt, popping attacks. Use the tip of your tongue directly into the reed's opening. Practice staccato on the reed alone to get rid of any pitch changes and any double sounds on the start or end of the note.

The big triplets should sound positively swashbuckling! Play with abandon and full-out dynamics!

WAYNE BARLOW - THE WINTER'S PASSED (1938)

Wayne Barlow, born in 1912 in Ohio, was a composition teacher at the Eastman School of Music, Rochester, New York, for many years. Although he wrote large-scale choral works and ballets, *The Winter's Passed* is his most famous work, and everybody loves it. You can also play the original version for oboe and string orchestra. This beautiful rhapsody is a perfect example of its type, American pastoral music of the 1930s and '40s: intimate, homespun, nostalgic, poetic. The *Pastorale* for Oboe by Howard Hanson is another example of this type of music, as is Copland's music for the motion picture *Our Town*.

The opening theme is forthright, honest and brave. It needs a shapely, arched downward slur from B to E (see downward slur advice in the Nielsen *Romance*) and very rich low notes. Make a nice crescendo to the poignant octave-E on your m. 3, and diminish to D. D and F are the notes that stick out most on the oboe; don't permit it! Try to play a beautiful, smooth line without any bumps from the fingers (see Elegiac

Dance for advice on finger action.) The tone needs fullness, body and sustaining power to convey the sturdiness, openness and pioneer spirit of the music.

This piece is a good place to cultivate really graceful attacks: clear, with a sort of poetic emergence and finesse. The attack should take nothing away from the tone. There should be forward motion in the attack, a nice flow like stepping onto a moving sidewalk at the airport. You take in your air, set your embouchure for stability, and put your tongue on the reed, just as string player would start with the bow on the string. We don't want to swat at the reed from a distance; that is too haphazard and uncontrolled. As you start to blow, pull the tongue away from the reed as the air is on the increase. Find just the right moment; if you wait too long and develop too much pressure, the attack will sound explosive.

A word about vibrato: it should confirm, not confuse the pitch and stay within the tone outline. Be especially careful on the note B, a note that tends to encourage too much vibrato. Vibrato is a gentle waving of the vocal chords, a sort of loud-soft pulsation, more than a pitch change. It is not supposed to make any noise in the throat.

It would be nice to play the whole first 8 bars in one breath, but do learn to take quiet, quick, unobtrusive breaths, and then you can breathe in many places without chopping up the music. At the end of the piece I did take a breath in the same phrase.

The really difficult part in this piece is the counting of the middle section, which is very syncopated (i.e. accents on beat 2 or 3.) You must feel each 8th note (or rest) in order to enter accurately. I strongly suggest penciling the piano notes as cues in your oboe part. Put an "x" where the short piano notes occur and other cues as well.

HINDEMITH - SONATA FOR OBOE AND PIANO (1938)
I. Munter ("Lively")

Paul Hindemith (1895-1963) was born in Germany, but he moved to America, taught at Yale (1940-53), and became an American citizen in 1946. Hindemith wrote a sonata for almost every instrument, including trombone, double bass, and harp. He also wrote several operas.

I have found in my years of teaching that many students have misconceptions about Hindemith and tend to play his music too heavily, neglecting the composer's lyrical, melodic qualities. Hindemith's style is "neo-classical" and "contrapuntal." That means he wrote complimentary, architecturally constructed, independent lines similar to Bach. Clarity and line are essential to bring out the counterpoint. The Oboe Sonata has nothing to do with the German army of WWII!

Let's look at the first eight-bar phrase. Try to achieve a really pleasing symmetry up and down, loud and soft, with the G on m. 6 as the high point of the phrase. The piano plays a light, waltz-like figure, that sounds like 3/8 time, sparkling and dancing. The oboe plays a contrasting melody in 2/4, going up as the piano goes down. Crescendo in the pair of ascending 8ths and again in the ascending pair of 16ths. Leave the E♭ open-ended, flaring into the rest to connect it to the A♭. Play the high A♭ as a pick-up note by up-swinging and tapering the end of it. Stress the following Gs and E♭s expressively, as appoggiaturas, the first G being the focal point of the phrase. In keeping with the dancing, sparkling mood, the 8ths are played short, even though there are no staccato dots.

The second theme (figure 3) is very lyrical, eager, and optimistic. Be sure the little notes are well sustained and do not drop out of the line. Play the G# 16th note passing tone in the second bar very generously. As in the first theme, crescendo the C# into the rest to connect with the next half of the phrase. The half-step motif (five measures before figure 4) becomes very important as the piece goes on. Play its first presentation very meaningfully. The stress is always on the first note; a broad, weighty accent from the wind, not primarily from the tongue! When an idea is repeated, use dynamics and try not to sound like a stuck record (figure 5.) Play the concluding half-step (figure 6) dramatically, "overloading" with lots of intense air.

After the fermata, the development begins very mysteriously, exploring that expressive half-step motif. Play the intervals with arched, vocal shape, and the motif meaningfully, as before. The music gradually becomes more urgent, more severe, ultimately insisting on the half-step, and breaking apart into syncopated, unpredictable entrances (before figure 10). Later, the second theme breaks forth in total joy, as if every church bell in town is ringing (figure 10). It concludes with a trumpet-like fanfare (the triplets.)

The symmetry and construction of the piece are very satisfying, but this is not dry music. I hope you will play it with lyricism, mystery, expression, and joy.

—Elaine Douvas

Pièce in G minor

Gabriel Pierné

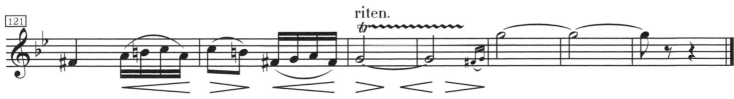

Concerto for Oboe and Strings
Preludio

Corelli-Barbirolli

Allemanda

Giga

Andante

3 ♩ taps
precede music.

Georg Philipp Telemann

Presto

Elegiac Dance

Oboe part edited
by Evelyn Rothwell

Michael Head

Poco più mosso *(dolce, poco rubato)*

molto rit.　　a tempo　　　　　　　　　　　　　　ritard.

Tempo Iº

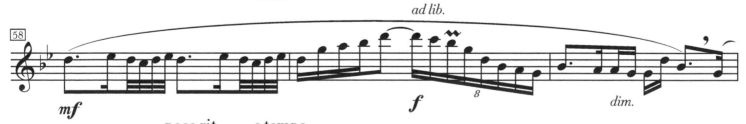

ad lib.

poco rit.　　a tempo

Presto

Oboe part edited
by Evelyn Rothwell

Michael Head

Romance

Carl Nielsen, op. 2

Humoresque

Carl Nielsen, op. 2

accelerando . . . .al . . . . Fine.

MMO 3412

The Winter's Passed

Wayne Barlow

Sonate - 1. Munter

Paul Hindemith

4 ♩ *taps*
precede music.

Munter (♩ = etwa 120)

Engraving: Wieslaw Novak